HAPPINESS HACK

Refine, Re-define, Hacking and Working on Happiness

James Barklay

Table of Contents

Introduction

In a survey conducted by a premier institution to find out what people are looking for in their present-day lives, it was not really surprising that 'HAPPINESS' figured prominently in the top three. A lot of us today are indeed looking for happiness. We speak about it at seminars and discussions, we might discuss it with our counselors, we also make it a common topic of conversation with our friends and family.

But the big question is — Do we <u>REALLY</u> know what happiness is?

That is actually where most of the problems lie:
- A lot of us equate happiness with contentment.
- We mistake materialistic pleasures for happiness.
- We might think that buying a new video game or watching a movie or even buying a car or a house is happiness.

In a way, these things might put us into a temporary state of felicity, but within a few short days, that feeling is gone. We are back to feeling exactly what we were before we got that particular object in our hands, and even start looking for the next thing that might make us happy.

However, we must note that **this is not** happiness at all. Surrounding ourselves with materialistic things that give us 'satisfaction' for owning that product, but it does not make us happy within. And that is the reason why it does not last long.

Chapter 1 - Refine Happiness

Before we begin, let us start with an important thought:

> *"Happiness does not come from the things we surround ourselves with. True happiness comes from within us, and it has nothing to do with our material possessions."*

Then, is having a good family or a relationship or being with friends true happiness? That does make us happy, doesn't it? But, once again, we must understand that these people can only make us feel contented. We feel great to have good people around us. However, no one — repeat, no one — can give us happiness. If you read the thought we have mentioned above, you will see that:

> *true happiness cannot come from any outside factor.*

The only place where it springs from is from within ourselves. There is no other source of happiness, and that's a truth you have to understand well.

What Is Happiness?

Happiness is an internal state of being. It is a feeling that tells us we have what we are looking for and we stop hankering for more.

By this definition, happiness does not mean a good house or a good job or a good spouse. Though these things might be important to us, they do not define happiness. The most important thing to know here is that happiness cannot be equated with such material things at all. We cannot pick up a bunch of things and say that this is what makes us happy.

Happiness is an accumulation of the feeling of fullness that we get from whatever we have, however, little or more it might be. Furthering this thought, it is possible that even a billionaire might not be happy because he is not satisfied with what he has. He needs more. That brings more torment to his mind. It is possible that he is troubled with all the billions that he has because he is insecure. He might worry that they might be taken away from him in some manner.

On the other hand, it is quite possible that a person living in a mobile house alone is truly satisfied. He does not want anymore and has no craving whatsoever.

Thus, happiness is a relative concept. There cannot be a single overarching definition of it that can apply to everyone. What is my happiness may not be yours.

It is for this reason that we need to find out own happiness. Even here, in this book, we can only tell you of ways in which you can pursue your happiness. But really getting that happiness should be solely your endeavor.

Here, we shall put down one more thought.

> *"Happiness is a choice. Everyone makes their own happiness."*

This is the summary of what we have spoken about so far. You are the only person who can choose to make yourself happy. No external factor can influence that. If you feel that any external element makes you happy, then that is temporal. You are only deluding yourself.

What Is Not Happiness?

The conventional line of thought suggests that a person who is happy has good things happening to them all the time. They think that real happiness is sunshine and butterflies at all times of life, come whatever. That is definitely not happiness.

Happiness is not about single episodes or incidents. All right, so you went on a picnic and it really gave you a very good feeling. But can we call that happiness? No. That's because that feeling will not last forever.

That is what life is about. As said in the acclaimed movie Forrest Gump, "Life is like a box of chocolates. You don't know what you will get." Life is the same. We do not know what is coming up next. But does that mean we cannot be happy forever?

That's far from the truth. A truly happy person will be happy even in the sad moment. Sounds ironic? You will not feel that way when you see what we have to say further. But it is true, a staunchly and really happy person will not be influenced by independent events. Yes, they might feel low for a while, but when the person had properly been conditioned to enjoy the good feelings of life, everlasting happiness can be found.

Perhaps all of this is sounding too clichéd and too rhetorical. Maybe we can explain things better by actually outlining the ways in which you can bring in the happiness in your life.

We shall now look at some ways in which you can bring true happiness in your life. Once again, these are only guidelines.

You have to put in the effort and make the choice.

Chapter 2 - Re-Define Happiness – Less Is More

It is extremely important for us to put a limit to our wants. The Four Noble Truths of the Buddha are as follows:

1. Human life is full of suffering. Suffering spares no one. The richest and the poorest all have to suffer in different ways.

2. All human suffering is caused due to desire. The desire of materialistic things is the root cause of all evil.

3. When this desire is eliminated, human suffering can also be eliminated. The more we can control desire, the more we can mitigate our own suffering.

4. To be able to achieve that, the person must follow a particular lifestyle. This lifestyle must include the right kind of speech, action, means of livelihood, effort, thinking, concentration, understanding, and resolve.

If we analyze these four truths, we can get a process by which we can create our own happiness. To reiterate what we have said before, happiness is not a standard. It varies from one person to another. It is because of this subjective nature of happiness that we have to build our own.

Consider a person who has always lived in a rural small town. He is quite happy with his life there and he feels he has enough for his living and even more. He does not hanker for more, and this gives him his happiness. But if he comes to the city and sees all the advancements there, and the increased features and facilities possible, he might feel inadequate. While he was happy in one place, he won't be in another. However, if he can condition himself to think that he does not require these gizmos, his life can be infinitely happier.

Wealth does not mean happiness. Having a large number of friends or a large family does not mean happiness. Jobs do not mean happiness. Being able to go out on vacations twice a year does not mean happiness.

> *Happiness is what you create for yourself — your personal level of satisfaction. It has to come from within you.*

Chapter 3 - Hacking Happiness

1. *Make a Positive and Firm Decision to Be Happy*

A lot of people around us are not happy because they do not have a firm resolution to be happy. These are the skeptics who think that there cannot be happiness in their lives forever. So the first thing that you have to do is **to intend to be happy**.

Make it a conscious choice.

Say to yourself, "I want to be happy." Say that over and over again. Maybe make a poster of it and paste it facing your bed so that it is the first thing you see every morning when you wake up.

When you do not get something that is genuinely your right, what do you do? Do you let it go? Do you sulk and slouch in a corner? Or do you make a firm resolution to get that thing and fight for it too if the need be?

Similarly, you must understand that being happy is your right too. You deserve to be happy. Even the Constitution offers us that. It is enshrined in the Declaration of Independence itself — "the pursuit of happiness".

So why give up? Happiness is your fundamental right.

> *Condition your mind to think that you deserve happiness and hence you should get it.*

You will see that this goes a long way to bring you your real happiness.

2. Assume Responsibility for Your Actions

Most of the sadness in our lives is because we depend on other people to make us happy. Someone who is unhappy at their job might blame their boss or their colleagues to make them feel that way. Someone who is unhappy in their relationship blames the other person or the circumstances. Someone who is not rich might blame the government. This goes on. We keep blaming people for making us unhappy.

But isn't this a sense of entitlement? Why should we give the strings of our happiness in the hands of others and dangle along like puppets? Why can we not take this responsibility upon ourselves?

This will begin when we start becoming accountable to ourselves. In everything that goes wrong, we should analyze what our role was in it. Could we have done things better? If a relationship has gone sour, we must think why it went so. Could we have helped it? Could we have done a better job so that the boss might not have reprimanded us? These are the things we must analyze.

When we condition ourselves to do such self-analysis, two things happen.

Firstly, we learn from our mistakes and know what not to do the next time.

Secondly, we gain a degree of confidence.

This confidence comes from the understanding that we know what went wrong and won't allow that to happen the next time. This is because we will hold the strings in our hands the next time and not give it away in the hands of other people around us.

3. Have a Proper Knowledge of Your Needs

One of the prime reasons why a lot of us are distressed today is because we don't really know what we want and how much of it we want. If it is a house, how big of it is enough to make it happy? Or a car — what features are enough to keep us satisfied with it? Even with relationships and jobs, we do not know how much we are actually expecting out of them.

It is human nature to constantly crave for more and more. Our minds are wired in such a way that we cannot ever be satisfied with what we have. If we achieve something, we are already looking for the next step.

We need to change this.

We need to sit down and think how much do we really want. The way to do it is to write down our requirements in a realistic manner and then try and stop when we have achieved those.

When we have a full realization of what we need to be happy, this could be our first major step towards really being happy.

4. Have Well-defined Goals

This is an extension of the above point. Once we know what can truly make us happy, we can jot down the goals we have in life. Our goals could be as high as we want, but they should be arrived at after a full realization of what we need to be happy.

> *Once the goals are made, ensure that they are non-negotiable.*

This goes both ways. If you have made a goal, you should try to achieve exactly that much, neither high nor low. There will be times where you might start craving for a higher goal, which might happen when you are actually closing in on your goal, but remember the time when you set down your goal. This is exactly what you needed for your happiness. Your current need to have something higher is delusional.

> *That is why it helps to write down things.*

When you have well-defined goals that you document, you won't feel the need to stretch yourself thin to achieve something higher. You will be contented with your achievements and that will put a constant smile on your face.

5. *Always Look for the Bright Side of Problems*

To quote a cliché, every cloud has a silver lining. But a cliché does not become a cliché unless there is some truth in it. And the truth in this one is quite profound — if you think about it, it is a very optimistic way of looking at things.

Being a glass-half-empty person never helps. If you read the lives of some of the happiest people on earth, i.e. those who have achieved what they set out to achieve, you will find that nothing every bogged them down.

It is not that problems did not arrive in their lives, but these people did not let the problems rule over them.

On the contrary, these people sat hard and thought — "Is there any way that I can deal with this problem?" Then they realized that the problem wasn't actually an impediment. In fact, it was a learning experience. There was something to learn from that difficulty, and they learned. This is what finally helped them get what they were looking for and brought the happiness into their lives.

6. Contemplate on Your Options

With anything that you do, there could be a dozen ways to approach it. For instance, you might want to get published as an author. Now you could do that the hard way, i.e. through publishing your book with a traditional publisher which uses a careful screening process. Or, you could self-publish yourself and reach a smaller audience but probably become famous too. Or, you could simply have a blog and publish your posts there. Whatever mode you choose, you are getting your name out as an author.

But, are you ready to be that flexible?

> *A lot of our problems are because we are too rigid in our ways.*

If one of us, for instance, wants to get published only through the traditional route and shut themselves to other options, then they are probably setting themselves up for a difficult time. So think about it. When you have easier options to achieve something, why do you go for the difficult ones?

Like, getting a high-flying job at the start is not possible most times. You should stop trying for that higher goal right at the outset. Instead, start with a lower profile at first.

Be ready to take up that option. It will give you more satisfaction. And if you are more satisfied with your current status, you will be more productive and probably reach that higher goal eventually.

7. Show Your Thanks to People

One of the things that is seriously wrong with most of us today is that we do not express our gratitude enough. Many of us plunge ourselves in self-infliction of hurt by thinking that we are surrounded by thankless people, but then think about it — do we show our thanks to deserving people enough?

We must make the start by expressing our gratitude first. And this applies to even the smallest person who does a service to us, even a paid service. Thank that cab driver for bringing you safely to your destination. Thank that elevator operator for pushing those buttons for you. Thank the waiter at the hotel for helping you out. Thank everyone and you will see the positive difference happen within your own life too.

The fact is that gratitude comes around.

When you begin to appreciate other's work, others around you are going to see it and emulate you too. It might take some time to come to terms with what you are doing, but it will happen eventually and you will see the ocean of difference that creates.

And when that happens, you will find appreciation coming your way as well, and this is one of the best ways to generate happiness in your life. Few things can make us happy as when our hard work is appreciated.

8. Do Not Be Selfish

Selfishness is the bane of our existence. We are inherently selfish, even as babies. We do not like to share things. We like to think of our own benefits. We want the best seats in the trains, we want the first position in a queue, we want the choicest morsels in a buffet, and so on. That's how we are.

But do you see how this can be so laborious? If we are always trying to hunt for the best of everything, we are always in a state of competition. That can never make us happy, can it? We will always be in a state of a rush because we want to overshadow others. This does not help.

> *Instead, if we can teach ourselves to share, we can be much, much happier. We have to learn to let go.*

What does it matter if we do not get that window seat in a bus or the best place in a theater? It does not change us one bit. It is all right if someone else gets that place. It is okay if we share what we have with others.

We do not really want the elevator all to ourselves. It is okay if someone else enters it with us. Such sharing will reduce the burden on our minds and help us reach a state of relaxation.

If you sit down and think how much we compete with others in our daily lives, you will very well understand how stopping that competitive nature can make us happy.

> *It might take some getting used to, but when you are accustomed to sharing, you will be much happier than what you are feeling now.*

9. Always Be Honest

How many times have you heard that honesty is the best policy? But how many times have you really applied it in your lives?

Now, honesty is not just about speaking the truth to others. It is also about presenting the true picture of what you are. It is also about speaking the truth to yourself.

If we camouflage ourselves with layers and layers of duplicity just to reach a certain standard of living that's set by the society around us, we are being dishonest.

If you try to be like others at the cost of losing your own identity, you are being dishonest to yourself. And such dishonesty can never give you happiness.

Once again, you will be in a constant state of war with yourself. You will always be competing your true self with the self you want to project to society. Can this make you happy? No. You might feel gratified for a while that you could fit in with the others, but it is not going to give you long-term happiness, and definitely not if you have to keep up a façade all the time.

Chapter 4 - Working On Happiness

To create happiness for yourself, you need to have self-realization. You need to know your goals and understand that selfishness does not help.

Here, we shall talk about some ways that you can start with right now to be happier from tomorrow itself.

1. Understand What You Value the Most

Set priorities. You are not able to achieve everything in this life. So, set goals to achieve the things that you absolutely cannot do without. Then focus your mind on achieving that. Obliterate the other things. Trim the fat. Without distractions, this will be much simpler than you think.

2. Do Not Hang on to Things that Don't Help You

Remove all the clutter in your life.

Get rid of all the things that you don't need. Remove all the memories of your failures; you don't need them. Give up on your old clothes, your old books that you no longer need, those trinkets in your house that are just using up space. Keep only the things that you really need.

Remember, less is more.

3. Chalk Out Your Career Path

Have a very realistic goal of what you want to achieve with your career. How far do you want to go? What do you want to achieve? Do you need to do other things? Such questions can help you build up a more fulfilling life. When you know your goals, peripheral things like your colleagues, your office space, the furniture, and even your boss will cease to matter.

4. Have a Clear Picture of the Home You Need

Yes, think about the home you need and not the home you want.

You do not want a palace to be happy.

The feudal lords who live in their mansions were never happy. Think about a small house that is enough for your needs and then fill it up with things that you really need. You will find that a smaller space really gives you more mental space.

5. Make a Checklist of Things You Want and Can Do Without

You need to assess what things you really need in your life and what you can do without. If you do not need those credit cards, get rid of them. Maybe keep only one. If you do not need that second car, sell it off.

Instead, build on more important things such as relationships. You will find that this goes a long way in bringing more happiness in your life.

6. Stay Away from Negativity

Negativity comes from some people around us. They could be our friends or our family members. Some of them can depress us to great limits. They can even put roadblocks in our performance.

For whatever it is worth, we take the words of our friends and family quite seriously, and most often these are the people who undermine our potentials. Familiarity breeds contempt, as they say.

So, sit down and identify the people who are bringing negativity in your life. Minimize contact with them.

7. Take Care of Yourself

Are you serious about your health? Do you exercise? Do you eat healthily? Bad habits can lead to stress and stress is the diametrical opposite of happiness. Try to do away with all these harmful elements in your life and take stock of your health and fitness.

Going for an early morning jog can really unclog your brain and make you look at the day with a fresher outlook. You owe to your body to keep it healthy, and once you do that, it will keep servicing you for a long time to come.

8. Applaud Yourself for Your Achievements

Think about what you have achieved so far. Count even the small happy things.

Maybe your child brought a certificate from school for a good drawing. Enjoy that. Celebrate that. Give yourself and your child a treat. You deserve it.

> *Make every happy thing an event to celebrate.*

Then you will unconsciously want more such occasions in your life to celebrate, and you will find them too. Your life will become a joyful celebration of small things that really matter to you.

9.   Stop Your Jealousy and Hatred

This will never help you. Wherever you go, there are going to be people who are more successful than you are.

> *From today itself, stop thinking about those people. Feel happy for them, if you must.*

10.   Write Down Your Three Wishes

This can give you a lot of happiness. Sit down with your family and let everyone write down the three things they want to achieve.

Then, as a group, try to achieve those. It is a great exercise too because you will get to know your family better. You could have a lot of laughs over these things, and these are the moments that you will cherish.

Conclusion

One of the most important things you must do to become happy is to take stock of the situation and not shy away from making any changes if they need to be made.

We have enlisted a lot of things in this eBook that you can do to bring happiness in your life, but if you not willing to make those changes, they are not going to work for you. For example, if you are not willing to let go of the junk that is accumulated in your life, you are not going to be proactive in seeking your happiness. If you are not able to keep away from things that bring negativity to your life, happiness is always going to be elusive.

You need to do these changes now.

Time is running out, and with each passing day, you are making happiness more and more distant from you. And, if you push back your own happiness, it will be more difficult to reach to it when you really want to.

So, be flexible.

You have to be open to your options and if something is not working out, make the change.

Often, the change is within you. Your happiness is just a reflection of what you are, so you will need to work those changes within yourself first to see it around you.

This was an insight on how we can create our own happiness.

> *Happiness is not a goal that you can achieve. It is not something that happens overnight.*

You need to work at it, bit by bit, but soon you will reach a stage where you will not have to worry about things anymore. By keeping worry away, you are inviting happiness in your life.

> *Share the happiness with others once you have discovered it. Appreciate the goodness in others. The more you find happiness in others, the more you will discover it within yourself.*

We hope this has been a good read. Here's wishing you a bountiful life full of happiness. Surge ahead and prosper!

Bonus Material

Get Free 5 (Five) " 50 Inspirational Quotes "

Total 250 Pictorial Quotes

Please visit http://bit.ly/1LfHSNx